fload

Mark Cunningham

Thanks to Linda Kobert, Christopher Simmons, harry k stammer, Amy Stephenson, and Mark Young.

The names of the mussels are given as they appear in *Missouri Naiades: a Guide to the Mussels of Missouri*, by Ronald D. Oesch, published by the Missouri Department of Conservation, 1995.

Parts of this book have appeared in *Otoliths*.

fload

(I)

Zebra Mussel

influx
in.flux
inflocks
inf.locks

Pink Paper Shell

iri.descent

Pink Paper Shell

stra.ite(m/n)ed

Pink Paper Shell

ligh

Pink Paper Shell

l/amp

Deer-toe

(a)isle

Zebra Mussel

byssail.abyssall

Pink Paper Shell

promirent

Deer-toe

scree(n)

1

Zebra Mussel

concavid

Deer-toe

poort

Pink Paper Shell

well separated
by connection

Zebra Mussel

them.theme

Pink Paper Shell

potamiliue

2

Pond-horn

oridgin

Zebra Mussel

enterfearing

Pond-horn

splattel
tralalas

Pond-horn

regular
transparent

Pond-horn

epidermiss

Zebra Mussel

coreall
corrally
core.all

Pink Paper Shell

laev

Deer-toe

durent.*dure*net

Deer-toe

substray.subray

4

Pond-horn

spateulate

Zebra Mussel

polymorefor

Pond-horn

dis.tend at (s/c)enter
only occupy
outer

Pond-horn

not minent.not
minute

Pond-horn

not great relief

Pond-horn

almost as

5

Zebra Mussel

musscle

Pink Paper Shell

varies by being
thinner, smaller,
less robust

Pink Paper Shell

varies by being

Pink Paper Shell

c/lose

Deer-toe

sporaidic

Deer-toe

(sp)litter.begend

Deer-toe

prizon

Zebra Mussel

pregnab
gene.rator.gene
ration

Zebra Mussel

fillter

Zebra Mussel

fasthold
(th)read

Zebra Mussel

trema
separabble
bail.last
momenthrum

(II)

Hickory-nut

capullary

Fragile Paper Shell

gap(ping)

Warty-back

divurgent

Pink Heel-splitter

anglion

Fat Pocketbook

turb

Pink Heel-splitter

rentaform

Fragile Paper Shell

fraygill.frag.gile

Fragile Paper Shell

denote.detone

Hickory-nut

rowd

Fat Pocketbook

ante.rovent

Warty-back

incurrved

Fat Pocketbook

ritch

Hickory-nut

co(a)sted

Fat Pocketbook

gravi(d)ty

Hickory-nut

obovious

Fragile Paper Shell

a mongrel.among

Hickory-nut

preferinse

Fat Pocketbook

(b)lind.unscene

Fragile Paper Shell

anchor(e)d.ored

Fat Pocketbook

unsu(r)d

Fragile Paper Shell

apres.hension

10

Hickory-nut

discharred
gravi

Fat Pocketbook

improp

Fat Pocketbook

rusty opening

Fat Pocketbook

no specialization
except for
a thickening

Fragile Paper Shell

pullp

Fat Pocketbook

metamor.epidare-
miss

Hickory-nut

papilloose

11

Warty-back

split.spilt

Fragile Paper Shell

picous

Fragile Paper Shell

insomuc(h)

Fragile Paper Shell

en(t/w)rench

Pink Heel-splitter

stands.till

Fragile Paper Shell

fee.bled

Warty-back

explain
ravall

Warty-back

drift

Fragile Paper Shell

disscoioccaizone

Pink Heel-splitter

distally

Warty-back

made of(f)
ex.tend

Pink Heel-splitter

erosion(w)ing

Pink Heel-splitter

ligul

Fragile Paper Shell

ousness.usness

Fragile Paper Shell

pho

Pink Heel-splitter

megapterus
metagap

Fragile Paper Shell

repsuredge

14

(IIIa)

Fawn's Foot

lea.ssh

Butterfly

clarift

Maple Leaf

tourbid

White Heel-splitter

ruddermentary
eros(e)ion

White Heel-splitter

marguniform

Fawn's Foot

unio zigzag:
f/ormiss

White Heel-splitter

abunch

Maple Leaf

conglut.inate

Maple Leaf

surcease.surdcease
crowdead

16

(b)

Pimple-back

may now be

Mucket

semi-ellitpi
undolater

Maple Leaf

heavein

Three-horned
Warty-back

scattered
extrud(g)e

Butterfly

actent

White Heel-splitter

comp.plan.at.a

17

Fawn's Foot

centrick

Mucket

filamomentous

*Three-horned
Warty-back*

ex(i)tending
ventrade
di-stance

Pimple-back

dridge

Butterfly

conflick

Pimple-back

dingy.ding.y

Maple Leaf

flapfoot

Mucket

central part
oblitterutted
between (l)oops

18

Butterfly

ventra(i)de

                                        Mucket

                                        lungetudinal

Fawn's Foot

openings. 0 penings

                                        Fawn's Foot

                                        occaizonal

White Heel-splitter

with age:
rayless

                                        Fawn's Foot

                                        t/runcilla

Mucket

cohesion.
when mature
coheshun

*Three-horned
Warty-back*

valva

*Three-horned
Warty-back*

grey.grayish

Mucket

nonym

Butterfly

cr.ease

Fawn's Foot

circuelar.
offset
in middle

White Heel-splitter

protuberinse

Pimple-back

salvague

Maple Leaf

(o/a)rborreal

21

(c)

White Heel-splitter

opening.
set.
thicky

Maple Leaf

plur

Pimple-back

a shallow sulc

Pimple-back

dent(r)ickle

Maple Leaf

diwrect

Fawn's Foot

semi*si*cular

22

Mucket

(st)rong

Pimple-back

ad.ob.solesence

Maple Leaf

marsoup

Mucket

suspecies
will require
more material

Butterfly

apeering

Butterfly

appairing

Three-horned
Warty-back

rid.gid
prminend

Mucket

seeptasacts

Fawn's Foot

spinel

Three-horned
Warty-back

reflecks.incur(v)
obliq aira

Three-horned
Warty-back

sterail
usually worn off

Fawn's Foot

confussed

Maple Leaf

pyl

Maple Leaf

sperse
s(p)lit
contwinue

Pimple-back

lister.b/last

(IV)

Yellow Sand Shell

somethingmess

Yellow Sand Shell

probeable hosts

Pistol-grip

course.coarse.
dimerge

Pistol-grip

undullations

Flat Floater

gall loop. gulp/nope?
sip honal
t(o)ureen/m

Flat Floater

held together by
co.oiled larvel
(th)reads

Pistol-grip

in media rest

Pistol-grip

lying flat:
stress

Pistol-grip

irregular ridges
rounded up

Pistol-grip

crenullations

Yellow Sand Shell

occlued

Yellow Sand Shell

true.fault

Pistol-grip

ob.leak

(Va)

Giant Floater	_Lilliput Shell_
backish cream	taxoplasma
Paper Floater	_Round Pig-toe_
w(at)te(a)r flo/at	cord.datum core.datum
Fat Mucket	
silolquoid.siloquoida	_Slough Sand Shell_
	graduall
Paper Floater	
white flecks exhibit occaison	_Fluted Shell_
	discernibble
	Giant Floater
Wabash Pig-toe	crink.led
impo(u)ndment	

Fat Mucket

sceen

Paper Floater

immeshed in an
angle.
un.it

Ellipse

outer half.
half of outer

Slough Sand Shell

monadd

Wabash Pig-toe

innerdg

Round Pig-toe

pleurob(l)em

Lilliput Shell

ext(r)eemity

Fluted Shell

unifor

30

Elk Toe

wayve

Giant Floater

llip

*Cylindrical Paper
Shell*

subtryangular.
secondary water

Paper Floater

outer, inner
almost same size

Wabash Pig-toe

dimissle

Snuffbox

inslide

Fat Mucket

salvoids

Slough Sand Shell

to.to*ward*

31

Ellipse

obloan

Giant Floater

rupt(o)uring

Lilliput Shell

separut

Cylindrical Paper Shell

irreg(ate)ular.
irregulat *or*

Snuffbox

obsoleap

Bullhead

discrete.vent
discretevent

Black Sand Shell

comb.ine

Monkey-face

sort *of*

Scale Shell

fis.sure

Britt's Mussel

fini.tite

Britt's Mussel

percollate

Elk Toe

squ.are

Bullhead

yphy

*Cylindrical Paper
Shell*

th/in.th/ing.

Lilliput Shell

lo.call
traveil

Fat Mucket

capillazy

Snuffbox

almost semi-

Snuffbox

somewhat remote
from outer

Black Sand Shell

concenstraytion

Scale Shell

minusth

Monkey-face

sigh lense
voi(c)d

Washboard

trapevoid
incur.rent

34

Washboard

irregulure
crassidense

Scale Shell

vestigall

Stout Floater

line nearly trait

Purple Pimpleback

rupst
scer oose
latereal

Ebony Shell

coar

Rock Pocketbook

invelop

Pink Mucket

lunel

Snuffbox

radiatoured

Snuffbox

rid.ges
margin.at(e)

Elk Toe

blip tighten

Snuffbox

travale

Paper Floater

slough down

Black Sand Shell

lensgth

Purple Pimpleback

imple

36

Rock Pocketbook

anteriadd

Paper Floater

end is a straight line

Pink Mucket

wi.despread

Monkey-face

metanerve.
metanever.
nerveer

Washboard

obt.use
gigan.tea

Rock Pocketbook

con/frag

Ebony Shell

spin(e)less

37

Ellipse

papiloose
numersouse

Bullhead

or cream

Scale Shell

adcesses
ce(a)ses

Paper Floater

spor raidic

Fat Mucket

common
*Notropi*s

Pink Mucket

insemilliptical

Stout Floater

t/weak

Lilliput Shell

tenta

Fluted Shell

co.arse

Ebony Shell

iforml

Black Sand Shell

latticesmal

Scale Shell

very faint

Paper Floater

white flecks
exhibiting occasion

Elk Toe

hinge.line

Snuffbox

diaph.rag dia.phrag
buried in (g)ravel

Stout Floater

phe*no*

Fat Mucket

plura.list

Ebony Shell

llel

Ebony Shell

valvuable

Rock Pocketbook

arccidents

Rock Pocketbook

twoburcurled.curled

                                   Pink Mucket

                                   or.b

Stout Floater

equell.
having medium

                                   Ebony Shell

                                   annulari(at)s
                                   no moor

(b)

Fluted Shell

Symphynota. heerd

Giant Floater

opaca.opaqua

Monkey-face

evalve

Fat Mucket

soilid

Wabash Pig-toe

fuse.con.shor/t/urn
subfall

Ellipse

centrod

Purple Pimpleback

stend

Round Pig-toe

abitarry

41

Slough Sand Shell

sloughdown

Black Sand Shell

gum.recto

Paper Floater

imbesillis

Monkey-face

connection
of outer
far removed

Elk Toe

macrodotuem

Bullhead

siphone

Elephant's Ear

stuffused

Elephant's Ear

valvue

Purple Pimpleback

x-uriant

42

Purple Pimpleback

cyc.lone

Britt's Mussel

outgulf

Britt's Mussel

f/lap

Scale Shell

f(r)acture
occaison.ally

Elephant's Ear

crossidents

Spectacle Case

invari.cracks
monodon't

Spectacle Case

longgate parallelram
length? usually

43

Round Pig-toe

omenclatter

Elk Toe

rusting(e)

Bullhead

c(a/o)ndense
confind
s(t)izo.stedi.on

Ellipse

(p)rivate

Elephant's Ear

ellip*to*

Slough Sand Shell

cr.ease

Britt's Mussel

tenebraid

Elephant's Ear

placentow

Scale Shell

pairish

Purple Pimpleback

abrup.tangle
concentrat\it

Fluted Shell

subtell

Giant Floater

notropis ignit
micropert

Wabash Pig-toe

ventrail

Monkey-face

marginull

Snuffbox

scalelop

Bullhead

inchire

Ellipse

re-leasing

45

Black Sand Shell

graveil

                                        Giant Floater

                                        pro.duct

Britt's Mussel

vacueity

                                        Pink Mucket

                                        eyespot not seen

Spectacle Case

evin(d)escent
pitt(s)ense
limph
(t)one

                                        Elephant's Ear

                                        unded

Scale Shell

de.*sic*.cation

Ellipse

steady ravel
ellips*i*form

Purple Pimpleback

o.pen

Fluted Shell

constet

Washboard

host: *I. nebulosus*

Rock Pocketbook

emerg.emarg.
(b)reach

Ebony Shell

micric

Spectacle Case

one. nearly in line

Spectacle Case

finit. it
unitarry. uniteary
shorel
fizz.sure

Elk Toe

manteledge

Ebony Shell

lengthth

Snuffbox

triquieter

Elephant's Ear

(l)oops
are
parallel

Black Sand Shell

longutudinal
extending

Spectacle Case

sp(re)ecull
sp(l)ored

Spectacle Case

blur.t

Elephant's Ear

fire.ring

Bullhead

bet.ween

Scale Shell

leptodent

Black Sand Shell

within.withthin

Pink Mucket

tuburr

Rock Pocketbook

fluvotile

Spectacle Case

marseepial:
compare *united*

Spectacle Case

ob.leak
oblickly forwards.
water len(d)s

(c)

Ellipse

elsewhere
has arrived

Britt's Mussel

permuconfronta
shun

Wabash Pig-toe

onglut

Round Pig-toe

morph.alogical

Elk Toe

ambl.blo.plite

Slough Sand Shell

more/moor
evoid

Lilliput Shell

thin (t)issues

Giant Floater

a.plod.in.not us

Britt's Mussel

branchaisle

Fat Mucket

midway
a.bout

Slough Sand Shell

err.oar
fl.apped

Lilliput Shell

runciled/runsilled

51

Britt's Mussel

un.dualate.bead

Wabash Pig-toe

ssimal.mall

Giant Floater

perca (f)lavescens.
lave scend.
evanesent

Monkey-face

undu.late.t/here

Slough Sand Shell

curthins

Washboard

(s)light
(s)lit

52

Monkey-face

in ex.tension/
b/lank

Paper Floater

wad/wade
delu(n)ge
surroam

Wabash Pig-toe

riable
addductor
fillame.fillaim

(VIa)

Three-ridge

probeably

Lady-finger

rawn up

Squaw Foot	*Pond Mussel*
la(r)val form	subrow.subs(r)atus. orerather

Pocketbook

chainge

Lady-finger

instunces

Squaw Foot	*Pond Mussel*
to lengthin or out	gestell.gestall

Three-ridge

occupried

Pocketbook

rid.ges

Lady-finger

som(e).a

Three-ridge

lea(k/f)
dist.ends

Three-ridge

inf(l)ect

Pocketbook

superseed

(b)

Squaw Foot

metamorphosis
in same manner
as _A. imbecilis_

Lady Finger

dialatatatata

Slipper Shell

epidermiss

Plea's Mussel

divergentarry

Neosho Mucket

b*lot*ch

Pocketbook

pinki(t)sch

Ozark Shell

errging

Pond Mussel

unbloan

Little Purple

ur.pull
urp.lull

Three-ridge

integragrit

Lady Finger

slig

Ozark Shell

obscued

Plea's Mussel

ril(l)ed

Plea's Mussel

disinterpursing

Little Purple

offten

Pond Mussel

unifor

Three-ridge

omenal

57

Neosho Mucket

containued.
a/gain

Ozark Shell

kin cyst

Neosho Mucket

pregnab

Slipper Shell

sh/allow

Pocketbook

with.draw.edgeded

Plea's Mussel

ellipsiformis(s)

Plea's Mussel

hecklist

Ozark Shell

cantdescence

Little Purple

toxolassoma

Squaw Foot

obalong

Neosho Mucket

discontint

Neosho Mucket

upside (d)own

(c)

Squaw Foot

longer than outer

Three-ridge

suboval

Plea's Mussel

wrink.led

Ozark Shell

arkens

Lady Finger

okaccasionally

Pocketbook

ventico(a)st

Three-ridge

pairsited

Ozark Shell

convex.caved

Plea's Mussel

struct

Slipper Shell

deltad

Lady Finger

gibbos
dialeek

Pond Mussel

blu(i)ish

Pond Mussel

(ob)lighterated

Little Purple

glans.euruncle

Squaw Foot

marsoupia

Little Purple

decimat.
deci.mate

Three-ridge

we(l)t

Squaw Foot

in/cite

Plea's Mussel

ongate

Lady Finger

comb.inations

Ozark Shell

irid

Slipper Shell

diagonal

Ozark Shell

thinner.(l)imply

Reeve's Mussel

indivi.duality

Reeve's Mussel

obtuss

Reeve's Mussel

micro.wager
micro.swagger

Pocketbook

bead.bulge.(p)inch
bluge.bluegill .

                                      Three-ridge

                                      elop(p)ed seepta

Reeve's Mussel

diagnoose

Neosho Mucket

(p)resent

Neosho Mucket

char(ged) ovisacs

(VIIa)

Kidney-shell

si(t/p)

Broken Ray

newtrall

Rainbow-shell

riadi*at*

Rainbow-shell

first proposed
for a genus
of flies

Asiatic Clam

negular s/pace

Broken Ray

incur.incurrent

Kidney-shell

some*what*

64

Rainbow-shell	*Kidney-shell*
post-half	lowcally
Broken Ray	*Asiatic Clam*
de-crease. ex-pand	sallilent
Western Fan-shell	*Plectomerus* *dombeyana*
both directions *out*	trapevoid
Plectomerus *dombeyana*	
elliptical *for*	
Western Fan-shell	
elongated into a coil	
	Rainbow-shell
	s(t)uffixed. s(n)uff.used

(b)

Purple Shell

ting lines

                                Western Fan-shell

                                ssh.allow

                                Little Spectacle-case

                                spectrummage

Broken Ray

spurst

Rainbow-shell

more blue

                                Asiatic Clam

                                innummerubble

Little Spectacle-case

val(v/u)e

Kidney-shell

inequip.par.trite

Little Spectacle-case

trans(v/w)erse

Western Fan-shell

starteruffle

Purple Shell

corruget

Rabbit's Foot

uni.orange
unio.range

Rainbow-shell

fact.or

Asiatic Clam

expansieve

Broken Ray

ne(u/a)r

Rabbit's Foot

margin somewhat
late

Asiatic Clam

abundont

Western Fan-shell

vurgent

Western Fan-shell

papillairy

                    Western Fan-shell

                    spots
                    dense enough
                    to form

Curtis' Shell

absencyst

                    Curtis' Shell

                    apostrophe nothing

                    Kidney-shell

                    interiorupted

Rainbow-shell

origedgedgination

                    *Plectomerus
                    dombeyana*

                    plycations

Little Spectacle-case

font.anus

Curtis' Shell

(g)loss

Plectomerus dombeyana

int.erred

Little Spectacle-case

bafal.
bfal

Curtis' Shell

oblivid

Rainbow-shell

multivasillation

Obovaria Jacksoniana

pressure.
un(st)able

Obovaria Jacksoniana

arest

(c)

Hickory-nut

scar.city

Broken Ray

numero.us
numerouse

Purple Shell

urpratus

Hickory-nut

host not listed
as inhabiting

Asiatic Clam

resiplocal

Little Spectacle-case

reprod.duct

Little Spectacle-case

biflowcull

70

Curtis' Shell

errunt

*Obovaria
Jacksoniana*

stoppage

Asiatic Clam

enterlocking

Curtis' Shell

exist

Purple Shell

muddell

*Obovaria
Jacksoniana*

er(r)osion

*Plectomerus
dombeyana*

inesse
inesse/ntial
inessensual
inessenshell

71

Also by Mark Cunningham

*Dented Breeze. Independently published.
(2023).*
Constelldriftongue. Independently published.
(2023).
bl(A)nk. Independently published. (2023).
morfact. Independently published. (2023).
sort/quantum. Independently published. (2023).
A Longer Life. Text with video by Dale Wisely.
(2022). YouTube.
<https://youtu.be/cSWPjndC7fM>.
Future Words. if p then q. (2020).
"f(l)ights." *Otoliths* 56 (Southern Summer 2020).
A 110-piece sequence. <www.the-
otolith.blogspot.com/2020/01/mark-
cunningham.html>.
"Fail Lure." *Otoliths* 52 (Southern Summer
2019). An 81-piece sequence.
<www.the-
otolith.blogspot.com/2018/11/mark-
cunningham.html>.
multizon(e). Text with video by Dale Wisely.
Right Hand Pointing. (2019).
<www.issues.righthandpointing.net/mul
tizone>.

Alphabetical Basho. Beard of Bees. (2016).
    <www.beardofbees.com/pubs/Alphabet
    ical_Basho.pdf>.

And Suddenly It's Evening. Beard of Bees.
    (2014).
    www.beardofbees.com/pubs/And_Sudd
    enly_Its_Evening.pdf>.

Regularly Scheduled. Beard of Bees. (2012).
    <www.beardofbees.com/pubs/Regularl
    y_Scheduled.pdf>.

Scissors and Starfish. Right Hand Pointing.
    (2012).

Helicotremors. Otoliths. (2012).

specimens. BlazeVOX. (2011).

nightlightnight. With photographs by Mel
    Nichols. Right Hand Pointing. (2009).
    <www.archives.righthandpointing.com/
    nightlightnight>.

71 Leaves. BlazeVOX. (2008).
    <www.blazevox.org/ebk-
    mCunningham%20REAL.pdf>.

80 Beetles. Otoliths. (2008).

Body Language. Tarpaulin Sky Press. (2008).

www.ingramcontent.com/pod-product-compliance
Lightning Source LLC
Chambersburg PA
CBHW032002060426
42446CB00041B/1248